who are you following?

PURSUING JESUS IN A SOCIAL MEDIA OBSESSED WORLD

FIVE SESSIONS

STUDY GUIDE FOR INDIVIDUALS & GROUPS

SADIE ROBERTSON HUFF

HarperChristian Resources

Who Are You Following? Study Guide

© 2022 by Sadie Robertson Huff

Requests for information should be addressed to:

HarperChristian Resources, 3900 Sparks Dr. SE,
Grand Rapids, Michigan 49546

ISBN 978-0-310-14892-0 (softcover)

ISBN 978-0-310-14893-7 (ebook)

HarperChristian Resources titles may be purchased in bulk for church,
business, fundraising, or ministry use. For information, please e-mail
ResourceSpecialist@ChurchSource.com.

First Printing May 2022 / Printed in the United States of America

contents

psst... start here.

Hey, hey!

You're here! Welcome, friend. The hardest part is behind you already, the part where you saw the title of this study and realized you might have some growth to do in this area of life and then actually *opened the book*.

Well done. It's a move you won't regret! How do I know? Because a few years ago, I, too, needed to grow in my ability to think more clearly about who I am following and to take courageous actions to better guard my heart, and the sessions you're about to experience reflect the very same steps I took.

why this study?

Let me say upfront that there is nothing inherently "wrong" with following people on social media, keeping up with your favorite influencers online, checking in regularly on a blog you love reading, and admiring people who are doing amazing things in the world. The Internet can be a great place to connect with friends, check out the latest trends, start a new business, and more. But if we're not careful, all that greatness can lead us astray.

We can start paying more attention to our screens than to the people in our real lives.

We can start trusting the voices of people we've never met over those who know and love us.

We can fall into the comparison trap, where every post we see is just one more opportunity to feel terrible about who we are, what we have, and how we're spending our days.

We can wake up one day and wonder how we've gotten so far off-course . . . how we've ended up somewhere we never intended to be.

The good news? The opposite is also true. If we *are* careful about who we're allowing to speak into our attitudes, our actions, our habits, and our lives, we don't have to be led astray. We can stay the course that God asks us to walk, the path paved by his acceptance and grace. That's where this study comes in.

study goals

In this five-session study, you and I will get honest about who we're following today and about where those influences are leading us. We will take a close look at what might shift in our lives if we were to be led by God's love instead of by strangers' likes. We will answer the tough question of whose glory we're really living for. We will learn how to come at our mistakes and missteps with divine perspective. And we will confirm once and for all where true fulfillment is found.

session segments

SEGMENT NAME	GROUP	PURPOSE
This Sesh	5 min	Brief overview of the session's content
Settling In	5 min	Stillness exercise to center your mind and heart before diving into the video
Roll Tape	15–18 min	Space to take notes on the video content that sets up the session
Whatcha Think?	30 min	Group questions to help you unpack the video content
Constructive Convos	10 min	Conversational opportunities to engage with the session content on a personal and practical level

SEGMENT NAME	GROUP	PURPOSE
Workin' It Out on Your Own		Questions to help you interact on a deeper level with the session's theme
Simple Steps		Actions to take between sessions to practice implementing what you're learning

Note: If you are reading along in the book, *Who Are You Following?* (Thomas Nelson, 2022), corresponding chapters for each session are noted just under the session's title.

s o l o   o r   g r o u p

This five-session study works both for individuals and groups. If you plan to go through the content solo, then consider reaching out to a friend or family member following each session to debrief your findings from that session. You might prep them upfront by saying, "Hey, I'm trying to be a little more intentional for the next few weeks about the voices influencing my life. Can I run some things by you as I go?"

As you work through each session, you may find the "Constructive Convos" segment especially helpful in initiating useful conversations.

c h e e r i n g   y o u   o n

I couldn't be more excited for you as you get going with these five sessions. Truly. God has such abundance in store for us, if we will just let his voice be the loudest voice in our lives! My prayer for you is that by God's grace you will know with fresh awareness that you are deeply loved, that you are thoroughly adored, and that you are purposed for good things in him.

know where you're headed

[Based on Chapters 1 & 2]

There aren't too many feelings that are worse than the feeling you get when you realize that somewhere along the way you made a wrong turn and ended up where you didn't mean to be.

—srh

this sesh

Read this quietly to yourself before getting started.

Where are you headed in life?

Big question, right? The question makes most of us pause. And honestly? It should.

Where *are* we headed in life?
And how are we heading there?
Blindly or intentionally?

In this opening session, we're going to sort out where we are today—emotionally, spiritually, intellectually, and habitually—and also declare where we want to be. We're going to look at where God says we *can* be, if we'll order our lives by his will instead of our own. And we're going to get real about which voices we're allowing to direct our steps—both online and in real life.

- Who is influencing what we think about?
- Who is influencing the opinions we defend?
- Who is influencing what we choose to be offended by?
- Who is influencing what we say, how we react, what we do?

The people we're following—that's who.

- Where are you headed in life?
- Where am *I* headed in life?

We're headed wherever the ones we're following are taking us. Where they go is where we will go.

settling in

Group leader, read this note from Sadie aloud.

If you're a Millennial or part of Gen Z—then you know that for us, life is a constant stream of input. And I mean *constant*. From the moment our eyes open each morning to the last blink before we drift off to sleep, we are absorbing and assimilating and assessing information, content, perspectives, opinions, ideas, posts, tweets, chats, feeds, and pins. It never stops.

Until now.

For the next three minutes, *stop the flow*. I know, I know: We can't *actually* stop the info flow from flowing. But we can turn away for a sec. And that's exactly what I want you to do. Set a timer for three minutes and hit start. Close your eyes and sit silently for the full hundred and eighty seconds. It will feel like an eternity—don't say I didn't warn you. But until we can be still, we can't know God. Psalm 46:10 encourages the same thing, that we just be still and know. And while I don't know your exact hopes and dreams for engaging with this study—we'll get to that here in a minute—I'm guessing that if you're here, then at least this much is true:

You really want to know God.

You've tried the other approaches to life, including trying to be God yourself, and nothing has worked so far. You figure, "Following Jesus is worth a shot." It is *so* worth a shot, my friend. However you can get to Jesus, my encouragement is to *get to him*.

So. Here's how we start: We start by being still. By coming into his presence with nothing in our hands. By simply sitting, and listening, and telling him we know he's near.

Ready?
Set?
Go.

roll tape

Watch the video for Session 1: "Know Where You're Headed" (about 15 minutes). Use the space below for your thoughts, notes, and quotes you don't want to forget.

Ending up in Eudora

Can't live without it

Social-media usage trends

> According to a recent Research study, people ages 25 to 40 spend an average of 2.5 hours per day on social media. For teens ages 13 to 18? It's closer to 7.5 hours each day.[1]

We'll go where the people we follow take us

Where are you headed in life?

Notes continued ▶

1 "Common Sense Census: Media Use by Tweens and Teens, 2019," Common Sense Media, accessed July 15, 2021, https://www.commonsensemedia.org/Media-use-by-tweens-and -teens-2019-infographic

Kingdom of this world/kingdom of god

Jesus, Jesus, Jesus

Becoming who we're meant to be

whatcha think?

Work through the following questions with your group (or on your own) based on the video you just watched. If you're short on time, choose to engage only with the questions that seem most relevant to you or your group.

Describe a time in life when you experienced the realization I mentioned in the video that "somewhere along the way you made a wrong turn and ended up where you didn't mean to be."

Maybe it was a wrong turn relationally. Or maybe it was a financial wrong turn. Maybe it was a wrong turn that you made on one dumb college night. Could have been regarding your career, your involvement in a local church, or yes, your use of social media.

What were the circumstances involved, and what did you do to recover, once you experienced that initial sinking sensation?

Obviously, a big determiner of where we're headed in life has to do with how well we manage our social-media involvement.

2

What did you make of the stats I cited regarding social media use today? Surprised? Not surprised?

☐ Shocking. Really. We all need to get a life—*fast*.

☐ Nothing shocking here. Look around! Every nose you see is all but Velcroed to a screen.

Where do you fit into the stats of 2.5–7.5 hours a day on social media if you're being honest?

Place an "X" on the spectrum below that represents the time you think you spend on your socials each day.

HOURS ├──┤ **2** ├──┤ **3** ├──┤ **4** ├──┤ **5** ├──┤ **6** ├──┤ **7** ├──┤ **8**

What do you typically do while online?

☐ Stay in touch with what friends are doing

☐ Stay up to date with news and current events

☐ Fill spare time

☐ Be entertained

☐ Network with other people

☐ Share photos or videos with others

☐ Share my opinion

☐ Research new products/services to buy

☐ Meet new people[2]

☐ Something else? _____

---

2 Monica Anderson, "A Majority of Teens Have Experienced Some Form of Cyberbullying," Pew Research Center, September 27, 2018, https://www.pewresearch.org/internet/2018/09/27/a-majority-of-teens-have-experienced-some-form-of-cyberbullying/

Talk about how it makes you feel being face-to-face with hard facts about our behaviors.

3 What did you make of the correlation I suggested between obsessive social-media use and effects on our mental health such as depression, loneliness, anxiety, and the chronic comparison game? Talk about any connection in your own life between social-media use and your mood.

In chapter 1 of *Who Are You Following?*, I talked about deleting the Instagram app from my phone for a time because I was "distracted by everyone else's lives and unhappy with my own." Distracted . . . unhappy . . . that's how I felt those days—can you relate?

4

If you had to name the top two or three feelings, emotions, or realities that social media brings to the surface for you, which would you pick from the list below?

☐ content	☐ joyful	☐ distracted
☐ envious	☐ prideful	☐ aware
☐ at ease	☐ generous	☐ informed
☐ curious	☐ awful	☐ angry
☐ bored	☐ eager	☐ jealous
☐ imaginative	☐ tired	☐ upset
☐ self-conscious	☐ wired	☐ peaceful
☐ others-focused	☐ energized	☐ grateful
☐ self-denigrating	☐ happy	☐ pathetic
☐ insecure	☐ unhappy	☐ involved
☐ secure	☐ focused	☐ seen

Talk about your choices and listen to each other—where we are all vulnerable and maybe stuck.

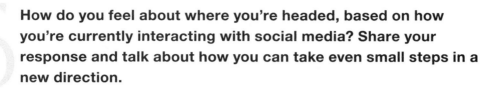

How do you feel about where you're headed, based on how you're currently interacting with social media? Share your response and talk about how you can take even small steps in a new direction.

☐ **I feel chaotic.** I haven't really sat long enough to think about the effects the online world has had on me, and my thoughtlessness is really starting to show.

☐ **I feel convicted.** It's probably time for me to make some long-overdue changes to my online habits.

☐ **I feel calm.** There's always room for growth, but I'm pretty careful about what I put in my mind and heart and reap the benefits of that intentionality most days.

When talking about the "other influences" we allow into our lives, it's easy to pick on social media. It's so *measurable*, right? We can measure how many of those influences we are following. We can measure how long we pause on a given post. We can measure the total time we spend being influenced. We can measure how much money all that influence gets us to spend.

But social media is hardly the only culprit here. For example, raise your hand if the following questions apply to you:

• Have you ever trusted the input of a podcaster you've never met over the input of a family member who's had intimate knowledge of your life?

• Have you ever put too much weight on a close friend's opinions, even at the expense of doing what you believed was right?

• Have you ever gone against your better judgment when making a critical decision because of something Google told you to do?

19

Before shifting gears to the next section, let's take a few minutes to talk about the loudest voices in your life today—online and IRL alike.

Mark the loudest voices in the list below:

- ☐ Friends
- ☐ Family members
- ☐ Professional athletes
- ☐ Actors and promoters

- ☐ Podcasters
- ☐ You Tubers
- ☐ Bloggers
- ☐ Vloggers
- ☐ TV personalities

- ☐ Columnists
- ☐ Professors/ Teachers
- ☐ Colleagues
- ☐ Pastors
- ☐ Authors

So, to whom are you listening?

Whose opinions and perspectives do you rely on?

Whose voice holds sway over your mind and heart?

To whom do you hand over decision-making power, and why?

Take a few minutes on your own and write down some honest observations you're making about yourself and hearing in others that you think could use some more attention, some deep thinking, and maybe some real change.

constructive convos

Read the conversation starters below, think through how you'd finish one or two of the sentences, and then take turns completing the sentences with the whole group. See if you can make it a few rounds. Be sure to carve out time for each group member to respond to at least one prompt.

Note: If you're doing this section solo, then consider having a few of the following conversations with family members, neighbors, work associates, or friends sometime this week OR just journal your responses in some alone time.

The essence of what makes me "me" is . . .	When I think about who I'm becoming, what comes to mind is . . .	The character quality I wish I had more of is probably . . .
Regardless of who I follow on socials, the kind of person I actually admire is . . .	How I'm feeling about Jesus these days? I'd say . . .	Between Jesus and "other influences," the one getting more of me lately is . . .
My biggest struggle right now is that I . . .	In my day-to-day life, I just wish I could find a way to . . .	What I wish my relationship with Jesus looked like is . . .

workin' it out on your own

Spend time on your own between videos and group meetings to work through some more personal questions.

1

**Let's do a little word association . . . you game? When I say
_____ , you say _____ .
Here are the topics; simply write down the first word that comes to mind.**

- When I say *time*, you say: _____

- When I say *habit*, you say: _____

- When I say *truth*, you say: _____

- When I say *beauty*, you say: _____

- When I say *God*, you say: _____

- When I say *socials*, you say: _____

- When I say *legacy*, you say: _____

- When I say *peace*, you say: _____

- When I say *purity*, you say: _____

Take a look at your responses to the previous question. What observations or insights can you draw about your train of thought?

Without even thinking too hard, where is your focus? What is most on your mind? Do you see a consequence, good or bad, to your focus?

Use the following list of characteristics or traits to fill in the blanks for each prompt.

caring	outgoing	questioning
free	responsible	afraid
authentic	wise	fearless
ready	truthful	impressionable
alert	fun	strong
serious	capable	easily-influenced
quiet	willing	engaging
helpful	respectable	selfish
accepting	a leader	selfless
generous	a follower	good listener
godly	reserved	faithful
fearful	defensive	thoughtful
kind	approachable	diligent
honest	distant	

What I think I'm known for now, by people who know me well:

_____   _____   _____

_____   _____   _____

_____   _____   _____

Remember: You are becoming who the people you are following are leading you to be.

4

This is the time to be honest. Because until we are honest about where we are at, we cannot get to where we need to go. When I stop to really think about the kind of person I want to be known as, a few qualities rise to the top of my list. For me those words are *faithful*, *authentic*, and *kind*. These are things I want to be known for.

What are those words for you? Write an honest list of what kind of person you want to be known as here:

- _____

  _____

  _____

- _____

  _____

  _____

- _____

  _____

  _____

- _____

  _____

  _____

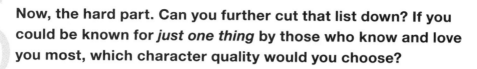

Now, the hard part. Can you further cut that list down? If you could be known for *just one thing* by those who know and love you most, which character quality would you choose?

Claim it in the box below.

Now, why do I bring all of this up, this emphasis on how we want to be known someday, on the person we hope to become? Because who we follow impacts how we are seen and known. If we aren't careful, if we don't decide for ourselves that we want to be known for being like Jesus, we risk being known for things we don't even like ourselves.

As we move into the final section—and throughout the four sessions to come—keep this singular character trait in the forefront of your mind.

simple steps

To close out session 1, I want to give you some simple steps you can take to either change direction toward Jesus or double check how much you are actually following the only good and true One worthy of your full attention.

Take a look at the ideas below and decide to give each one a try. You might even write them on your daily calendar so that you won't forget to prioritize them this week.

☐ **Begin each day in prayer.** As in, before you reach for your phone to see what the world is up to, spend your first moments with your heavenly Father to see what *he's* got going on.

☐ **Memorize Hebrews 12:1–3.** (See the quotebox on the next page.) If you've never memorized Scripture before, it's not near as hard as you might think. In John 15:5, Jesus says this: "If you remain in me and I in you, you will bear much fruit; apart from me you can do nothing." And one of the main ways we can "remain in him" is by saturating our lives with God's Word. As you work to memorize this passage, pay careful attention to the phrase, "fixing our eyes on Jesus." Ask yourself throughout your days here and there, "Are my eyes fixed on Jesus, or are they fixed on this new trend, that new update, this influencer's post, that friend's rant?" If anything but Jesus is your answer, fix that fixation fast. Ask God to help you, friend. God loves when we fixate on him.

> Therefore, since we are surrounded by such a great cloud of witnesses, let us throw off everything that hinders and the sin that so easily entangles. And let us run with perseverance the race marked out for us, fixing our eyes on Jesus, the pioneer and perfecter of faith. For the joy set before him he endured the cross, scorning its shame, and sat down at the right hand of the throne of God. Consider him who endured such opposition from sinners, so that you will not grow weary and lose heart.
>
> — Hebrews 12:1–3

☐ **Get real with a friend or family member.** Reach out to two or three people you trust and have a straight-shot conversation with each one. What do they observe about the people in life you are listening to the most? How would they articulate what it seems like your priorities are? Do they ever hear you talk about your spiritual beliefs? Do they know what you think about God? Choose a few of the "constructive convo" topics from page 21 of this guide and see what those chats reveal.

☐ **Make a list of (non-device–related) loves.** What do you like to do, apart from scrolling socials? Christian and I love to dance. I love to read. Play with my daughter, Honey. Have game nights with friends. Have family movie nights. And play tennis. Now, it's your turn. In the space below, jot down as many pastimes as you enjoy passing time with. Remind yourself of what you used to do, before phones and screens captured all our free time.

29

Things I love to do when I'm not online . . .

1 _____

2 _____

3 _____

4 _____

5 _____

6 _____

7 _____

8 _____

☐ **Push pause.** You knew this was coming, right? Carve out a window of time each day this week when you aren't attached to your phone . . . or your iPad, or your Kindle, or your laptop, or whatever device keeps distracting you, or worse, keeps leading you. Stick it in the upstairs bathroom, set an alarm on your watch to go off after the amount of time you hope to abstain, and then go about your life.

What do you notice about your attitude, your perspective, your heart rate, and your level of engagement with the outside world when you're not allowing random unchecked influences to lead you? Journal about your experience following your heart, your spirit, your truer self here:

choose love over likes

[Based on Chapter 3]

We can live as ones who are divinely loved instead of straining for likes. We can live as ones who may be different by the world's standards but who *fit right in* with God. We can live as ones who are far from disregarded . . . no, we matter deeply in the kingdom of God. We can live as ones who have never been disdained a single day in our lives.

—srh

this sesh

Read this quietly to yourself before getting started.

Do you believe that God loves you? I mean *really and truly* loves you?

In this second session, we'll take a look at what happens when you and I live like women who are loved by God. In the same way that when we refuse another person's love, we stop that relationship from being able to grow, when we don't allow God's love to penetrate every aspect of our being, our intimacy with him totally stalls.

Here's a question: What might change for us when we take God at his word that he adores us, that he esteems us, that he considers us *beloved*? How might we deepen our knowledge and experience of God when we allow his love to come our way?

settling in

Group leader, read this note from Sadie aloud.

Before jumping into the video portion of this session, I want to invite you to begin the way we did last time—in perfect silence before God. (How did it go for you then, by the way?) Being perfectly still and perfectly silent can feel freakishly awkward, I know. It is such a departure from how we are accustomed to spending our minutes, our days, and our lives. But the benefits are undeniable. God knew this was the case! Why else would he outright *command* us to be still and to know that he is God?

Beginning with this session, I'll be giving you a topic to think about as you sit quietly for the three-minute span. You don't have to focus on this topic, of course, but if you found last time that you had trouble keeping your mind from wandering to things that you can wait until later to address—your to-do list, your craving for a latte, the decision on what you're going to wear to tonight's thing—then this part is for you.

Did you know that for thousands of years—ever since David was king—lovers of God have carved out times throughout their day to simply sit quietly in the presence of God? Down through the ages, people just like us have stopped the flow of their days, come before God, and decided to wait on him. They figured that to have an intimate relationship with their Father, they needed to communicate with him. And so they'd sit. And think. And wait.

God usually had something to say.

Now, to you: If you need a way to keep your attention trained on God for these three minutes, consider focusing on the topic of this session—*love*. Specifically, *God's* love. More specifically, God's great love for you!

Romans 5:8 says, "But God demonstrates his own love for us in this: While we were still sinners, Christ died for us." As you sit in God's presence now, consider silently repeating one of the ideas from this verse. A few phrases that you might try include:

- ☐ You demonstrated your love for me.
- ☐ Your Son died for me.
- ☐ You loved me so much that you sent Jesus to die for me.
- ☐ You loved me in spite of my sin.
- ☐ You love me!
- ☐ I love you, Lord.

Choose one of the options above or come up with your own. The idea is just to think this thought again and again, turning it over in your mind, for the entire three minutes. If your mind wanders at some point, gently direct your thoughts back to that phrase.

All right.

Timer set for three minutes?

You
May
Begin.

Sadie

roll tape

Watch the video for Session 2: "Choose Love Over Likes" (about 17 minutes). Use the space below to log your thoughts, notes, and quotes you don't want to forget.

What we say and do to be liked

Being "likable" in relationships that matter to us

The connection to fear

Approval-seeking is always motivated by fear. We're afraid that we'll be seen as different—that we won't fit in. We're afraid that we'll be disregarded— that our lives won't matter. We're afraid that we'll be disdained—that we will be deemed unworthy of attention or love. Stressing over what others think of us will never lead us to the life of our dreams.

Living as ones divinely loved

"Daughter, your faith has made you well"

What's broken in you today?

whatcha think?

Work through the following questions with your group (or on your own) based on the video you just watched. If you're short on time, choose to engage only with the questions that seem most relevant to you or your group.

What came to mind for you when I asked what you've said or done so far today just to be liked? Any actions or interactions pop to mind when I mentioned these typical ways we strive for likes?

☐ Saying something to someone I didn't really mean, just to gain their approval

☐ Making a choice I normally wouldn't make, just to please someone else

☐ Presenting a fake version of myself, just to get a like

2
What's the difference in doing something to genuinely be kind
and doing something just to be liked? Where is the line between
the two, and how do you know when you've crossed it?

3
How well did you relate to my story about Christian's and my
dating days? Describe a relationship you've been in when
eventually you were incapable of keeping the "real you" from
seeping out. What were you afraid might happen, when the other
person got to know you, as you really are?

4   I introduced three fears that I believe motivate our longing to be liked, which I've listed again here. Which of the three have you experienced most often? Looking back into your life, where do you think this fear came from? Select one fear from the list below, and then write about its "origin" in the space that follows.

☐ The fear of being seen as different . . . of not fitting in

☐ The fear of being disregarded . . . of your contribution—or even your life—not mattering

☐ The fear of being disdained . . . of being seen as unworthy of attention or love

5   What did you make of the apostle Paul's promise that as you and I grow in spiritual maturity, we'll no longer be "tossed about" by what other people think of us?

If I could sit across from you right now, the thing I'd love to know your perspective on is that story I brought up in the video from Matthew 9, the one where the ailing woman boldly touched the hem of Jesus' garment in hopes of being healed. What do you think of Jesus' response that her faith is what made her well?

What feels broken in your life today that you wish could be healed by faith?

☐ **Does your life's *purpose* feel broken these days?** Purpose anxiety is a whole *thing*, you know. If this is you, you're not alone.

☐ **Does your *faith* feel broken these days?** Doubt can be a robber—of contentment, of livelihood, of joy.

☐ **Does your *physical body* feel broken these days?** The woman in Matthew 9 must have surely felt this way.

☐ **Does a *key relationship* feel broken these days?** It can be agonizing to be at odds with someone we adore.

☐ **Does your *money situation* feel broken these days?** Lack of financial resources can make all of life feel hard.

☐ **Does your *career* feel broken these days?** Feeling stalled in our work life can make us start believing we have nothing of value to add to the world. Such a miserable place to be.

☐ **Or maybe it's something else entirely . . .**

_____

_____

Brokenness is challenging because brokenness raises fears in our minds. The fear that we're all alone in the world. The fear that we are unlovable. The fear that we won't make it in life. The fear that the chronic pain will never get resolved. The fear that we'll never do anything impactful. On and on it goes.

With your answer to the previous section in mind, what fear does the brokenness you're facing today bring to the surface for you?

To *all* forms of brokenness, Jesus says, "You can be made well."

To *all* forms of fear, Jesus says, "My love is stronger still."

Read the words of 1 John 4:18 in the quotebox, filling in the blanks on the next page as you go. Then, jot down a prayer to God on the lines that follow, asking him to overshadow your fear with his love.

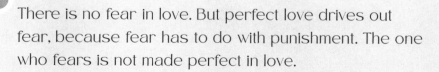

There is no fear in love. But perfect love drives out fear, because fear has to do with punishment. The one who fears is not made perfect in love.

—1 John 4:18

43

"There is no _____ in _____ . But perfect

_____ drives out _____ , because

_____ has to do with _____ . The

one who _____ is not made _____ in

_____ ."

Dear God,

_____

_____

_____

_____

_____

_____

_____

_____

_____

_____

_____

_____

_____

In Jesus' name, Amen.

constructive convos

Read the conversation starters below, think through how you'd finish one or two of the sentences, and then take turns completing the sentences with the whole group. See if you can make it a few rounds. Be sure to carve out time for each group member to respond to at least one prompt.

Note: If you're doing this section solo, then consider having a few of the following conversations with family members, neighbors, work associates, or friends sometime this week OR just journal your responses in some alone time.

What I've done, to try to be liked? Well, for starters . . .	Do I believe that Jesus can satisfy my need to be liked? I'd say . . .	I want to be seen as relevant because . . .
The types of messages my heart doesn't need are . . .	Who I seem to be, when I'm in good lighting is . . .	Who I really am, regardless of how I appear, is . . .
When I've struggled to feel loved by God, it's been because of . . .	I'd say the percentage of time I share my true self with others is about . . .	Between attracting followers or friendships, I'd say I work harder at . . .

workin' it out on your own

Spend time on your own between videos and group meetings to work through some more personal questions.

In today's world, we know exactly how to be liked. We know the right words to use. We know the right filters to use. We know the right percentage of *people we're following* to *people who are following us* to maintain. We know the names to drop in casual conversation, the events to be part of, the on-point shoes to be wearing in a given post.

True?

What are some lessons you've learned along the way about how to be liked in the world in which we live? (Never post an unfiltered pic, anyone?) Jot down a few that come to mind, and then, if you're working through this study with others, share your best tip with those in your group.

LESSONS ON HOW TO BE LIKED: PRO TIPS I'VE PICKED UP
1
2
3
4
5
6
7

The trouble with investing ourselves in racking up likes? Those likes are at most a fleeting high. Once we add a "like" to the mix, we raise the bar on how many likes will satisfy us and then have to go hunting for more and more likes. It's a vicious cycle . . . a game we'll never win.

Need proof of this dynamic? Here's a quick, two-question exercise:

1. How many followers do you have today on whichever platform you use most? _____

2. How many followers do you *want* to have? _____

Just out of curiosity, did you list the same number for both answers?

You didn't, right?

Why? Because nobody does. Those answers will never, ever match, because when it comes to garnering other people's praise, enough is never enough.

Ready for a far better way to invest ourselves?

It has *nothing* to do with positioning ourselves to capture likes from other people and *everything* to do with positioning ourselves to be captivated by the God of love.

That's not a bad mission statement for life, incidentally: "to be captivated by the God of love."

You can borrow it, word for word. I'm more than happy to share!

Now, let's talk about how to become captivated by the God of love.

What practical moves can we make?

Whenever our goal is to be "captivated" by another, three key habits are always at work: proximity, authenticity, and frequency.

1. **Proximity:** you get *around* the other person

2. **Authenticity:** you get *real* with the other person

3. **Frequency:** you get *consistent* with the other person

You get around them. You get real with them. You get consistent with them.

What do you get from all this getting?

Intimacy:

> Being seen.
>> Being known.
>>> Being loved.

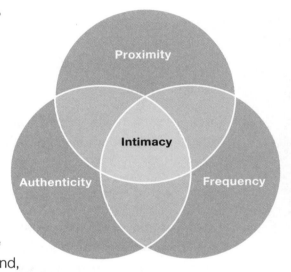

In my relationship with Christian, I told you that we spent the better part of two months talking by phone before we ever went out on our first date. And while I don't regret a single minute logged getting to know his mind, his heart, and his priorities on those calls, that phone-based approach wasn't going to serve us forever. Why? Because a key part of intimacy is ***proximity***.

Similarly, once we started dating in person and I could look amazing for the four or five hours we'd be together, eventually the real me started to show. Eventually, he saw who I really was, which was totally necessary, if we hoped to move forward in our relationship. Why? Because a key part of intimacy is ***authenticity***.

And finally, as in every healthy dating relationship, because Christian and I longed to further deepen our connection, we started hanging out all. the. time. Something in us knew that for us to experience true intimacy, *frequency* would be part of our deal.

But what does all of this have to do with positioning ourselves to be captivated not with a boyfriend or husband, but rather with the God of love?

The habits remain the same!

If you want to be in an intimate relationship with the God who made you and loves you, then you will prioritize with him:

- **proximity**—drawing near to God, as Hebrews 4:16 says to do
- **authenticity**—coming clean about our struggles and sin, as 1 John 1:8 tells us to do
- **frequency**—seeking God's kingdom before anything else, as Matthew 6:33 reminds us

What might this look like for you? See if you can connect each intimacy habit on the left with its corresponding commitment on the right. Draw a line from the habit to the commitment, below.

Proximity

"I'll spend time with God every day, not just when crisis strikes."

Authenticity

"Instead of settling for second-hand faith, I'll have my own personal relationship with God."

Frequency

"I'll tell the truth about my current struggles to God. He knows the truth, anyway!"

With these three aspects of intimacy fresh in your mind, which one would you say comes easiest for you? Which one has proven most difficult? What might shift in your mind and heart if you were to start equally prioritizing all three?

Capture your thoughts on the lines below before moving on to the final segment.

_____

_____

_____

_____

_____

_____

_____

_____

_____

_____

_____

_____

_____

_____

_____

simple steps

To close out session 2, I want to give you some simple steps you can take to begin implementing your newfound awareness of how often you're living for others' likes versus living from a place of being loved.

- ☐ **Notice when you're striving for likes.** Throughout each day, ask yourself, "Am I saying or doing or posting this *to be liked* or from a place of *being divinely loved*?" If you're unsure, then you may find it helpful to glance back at page 42 in this guide. Is what you're about to say/do/post reflecting one or more of those character traits you say you want to be known for? If not, consider foregoing that word, that action, that post.

- ☐ **Read 1 John 4:18 each morning.** (See quotebox.) Begin your day by saying aloud the opening words to this powerful verse: "There is no fear in love." Thank God for this truth. Ask him to drive out whatever fears you woke up with. Tell him that you long to live today "made perfect" by his perfect love.

> There is no fear in love. But perfect love drives out fear, because fear has to do with punishment. The one who fears is not made perfect in love.
>
> —1 John 4:18

- ☐ **Prioritize intimacy with God.** Come near to God. Be real with God. Each day.

get glory for God

[Based on Chapters 4, 5 & 6]

God wants to be our "just one." Wait, that's not strong enough. God *demands* to be our just one.

—srh

this sesh

Read this quietly to yourself before getting started.

Whose glory are you living for right now?

Ouch, huh?

There's a question!

As much as you want to say you're living for God's glory, I challenge you to really ask yourself if your life is being lived to bring him glory.

I probably don't have to tell you that for people in my age group—maybe yours, too, if you're age 18 to 25—the desire for fame is our number-one life goal these days. (Some studies showed that it ranked as our number two. Either way, that is serious!)

My opinion is that "fame" isn't the problem. The problem is that *we want that fame for ourselves.*

In this session, we'll look at what it takes to shift our priorities from wanting to gather glory for ourselves to focusing all our efforts on gathering glory for God. Let's look at this together and reshape our desires for the things that matter.

settling in

Group leader, read this note from Sadie aloud.

As we get going, let's resume our practice of sitting still before God for a full three minutes' time. Was this experience easier for you last time, or were you still itchy to chat with someone or check your phone? No judgment here, friend! I ask only that you stay the course for these five sessions, engaging with each element so that in the end you can piece together a go-forward strategy that works for you.

All right: Let's look at our topic for this week. Again, if you want to just sit silently and think about nothing in particular, go for it. But if you'd like a scriptural focal point, read on.

Our subject this week is *God's glory*, and a passage I have always loved along these lines is Psalm 19:1–4. Here is what those verses say:

> *The heavens declare the glory of God;*
> > *the skies proclaim the work of his hands.*
> *Day after day they pour forth speech;*
> > *night after night they reveal knowledge.*
> *They have no speech, they use no words;*
> > *no sound is heard from them.*
> *Yet their voice goes out into all the earth,*
> > *their words to the ends of the world.*

It's such a beautiful image, isn't it, the thought of the heavens praising God, declaring God's goodness, gathering up glory for him? Feel free to create a word or phrase from this passage on your own, or else pick from the ones that came to my mind, below:

- ☐ The heavens declare your glory!
- ☐ You deserve all the glory.
- ☐ The work of your hands is praiseworthy.
- ☐ You are good.
- ☐ You are worthy of all glory.
- ☐ I live to bring you glory.
- ☐ All the earth praises you, God.
- ☐ Praise
- ☐ Glory
- ☐ Worthy

Once your timer is set for three minutes, go ahead and tuck that phone away so you're not tempted to peek at it.

Still your mind and body and Begin.

Sadie

roll tape

Watch the video for Session 3: "Get Glory for God" (about 14 minutes). Use the space below to log your thoughts, notes, and quotes you don't want to forget.

David v. Goliath: a recap

A story with some *crazy* turns

God's kingdom, not ours

> It's *God's* kingdom we're trying to build, not ours.
> It's *God's* power we're longing to lean into, not ours.
> It's *God's* glory we're trying to gather up, not ours.

Notes continued ▶

Envious of what everyone else has

So distracted by her life that you miss your own

Let's be jealous only for God's glory

Trees planted by streams of water

Be like that tree in Psalm 1. Plant yourself beside God, friend. Quit fighting for your own advancement. Greatness belongs to God, alone.

whatcha think?

Work through the following questions with your group (or on your own) based on the video you just watched. If you're short on time, choose to engage only with the questions that seem most relevant to you or your group.

1 **The story of David and King Saul is a wild one, isn't it? And yet that theme of wanting what someone else has is one you and I both can relate to. When have you felt jealous or envious of another person's success, and why do you think those feelings emerged? Describe the circumstances involved below.**

2 Most likely, you didn't take Saul's tack of hurling a spear at or putting a hit on the person you were jealous of. And yet if you're anything like me, jealousy can bring out the very worst in you. How would you describe the sensation of being envious of the life someone else is living? How does envy make you feel? (This may get messy, but just get it out there. It is so important that we know how we are acting.)

3 I mentioned in the video that while you and I would probably never say these things aloud, falling prey to the comparison game equates to our lobbing silent questions at God:

- Where is *my* platform?
- Where are *my* follows, *my* likes?
- Why aren't people commenting about *me*?

What questions would you add to the lineup here, that "comparison" makes you ask?

- _____
- _____
- _____
- _____

In the video, I talked about the fact that God is jealous for our attention and then posed the questions, "But why? Is God some kind of crazed narcissist who's trolling for some positive PR?" I then explained that God isn't narcissistic at all. Rather, he knows that when you and I spend endless hours mindlessly comparing ourselves to other people and entertaining jealousy over the lives we believe they live, underneath those habits is a desperate attempt to rack up glory for ourselves.

How does this line of thinking relate to your firsthand experience? True for you? Not what you've seen play out? **Do tell.**

5

Check out what the following verses have to say and log the themes you find there.

SCRIPTURE PASSAGE	THEME(S) COVERED HERE
Mark 7:21–23	
Amos 4:13	
Isaiah 55:8–9	
Proverbs 28:26	
Isaiah 40:28	

How do you think these themes help explain why God wants glory for himself, alone?

6 You know how I love that image of the tree planted by streams of water, from the opening lines of Psalm 1. Reread the full passage in the quotebox, and then consider this: What do you think the "tree" and the "streams of water" represent, and why?

What four actions does the passage say are involved in being planted by streams of water?

Can the tree survive without the streams of water? What do you think? And what does your answer have to do with God receiving glory in and through our lives?

> " Blessed is the one who does not walk in step with the wicked or stand in the way that sinners take or sit in the company of mockers, but whose delight is in the law of the LORD, and who meditates on his law day and night. That person is like a tree planted by streams of water, which yields its fruit in season and whose leaf does not wither—whatever they do prospers.
>
> — Psalm 1:1–3 "

constructive convos

Read the conversation starters below, think through how you'd finish one or two of the sentences, and then take turns completing the sentences with the whole group. See if you can make it a few rounds. Be sure to carve out time for each group member to respond to at least one prompt.

Note: If you're doing this section solo, then consider having a few of the following conversations with family members, neighbors, work associates, or friends sometime this week OR just journal your responses in some alone time.

I think that security or confidence in who we are comes from . . .	The part of my life that I feel most insecure about these days is . . .	The thing that my current insecurity keeps me from experiencing is . . .
Do I believe that intimacy with Jesus can help me feel secure? I'd say . . .	The part of me that was obviously formed by God is . . .	The part of me that I have trouble believing was formed by God is . . .
The self-talk I speak over myself that reflects that I am wonderfully made is. . .	The self-talk I speak over myself that doesn't reflect God's love for me is. . .	I'm most tempted to care more about "looking good" than "living good" when . . .

workin' it out on your own

Spend time on your own between videos and group meetings to work through some more personal questions.

I want to walk you through a three-phased sequence you can practice anytime you're struggling with jealousy over someone else's situation, stuff, or life. Let me give you all three phases first, and then we'll practice moving through each of them in turn.

Phase I: "That is so awesome for them."

Phase II: "God, thank you for . . ."

Phase III: "I choose to delight myself in you."

Here's how these phases work:

Whenever you catch yourself saying (or thinking), "Wow . . . that is so awesome for them that they get to _____," (that's phase I), instead of spiraling down into an abyss of comparison, self-loathing, and resentment toward God, choose to take a different tack. This brings us to phase II.

Choose instead to say, "God, thank you for _____," filling in the blank with a blessing you see in your life. Could be a good friend that came over to hang. Could be your daughter's sweet smile. Could be the pup resting at your feet. Could be the fact that you're having a pain-free day. Whatever it is, pause and thank God for it aloud. On to phase III.

Phase III is this: *Choose to replant yourself in the Lord.* Thank God and then replant yourself in his presence, in his power, in his perfect provision for your life. He *is* near, you know. His strength is at hand. And the Bible promises us in Psalm 37:23 that "the LORD directs the steps of the godly. He delights in every detail of their lives" (NLT).

Ready to practice?

Yeah. Me, too.

First up: Think of a recent occasion when you felt envious of someone else's something. Her custom home. Her lavish vacation. Her cute clothes. Her solid marriage. Her perfect brows.

Have something in mind? Write it here:

_____

_____

_____

Next, shift your gaze from that person's coveted thing to something in your own life you're grateful to God for.

Something come to mind? Write it here:

_____

_____

_____

Incidentally, let me pause you here and ask you to reflect for a beat on the emotional swing we experience when we intentionally shift from greed to gratitude. Did you feel it as you forced yourself to name something you're thankful for? How would you describe that emotional shift? Put words to it in the space below.

Now, to the replanting phase. From that place of gratitude, thank God that by his Spirit, you can be replanted from envy to enthusiasm for his goodness, from covetousness to confidence in his power, from jealousy to genuine peace. Ask God to remove every last ounce of fear, frustration, resentment, and spite from your being and to replace those things with clear-cut evidence that his Spirit has captured your heart. The enemy would love to make you feel like you are a hypocrite for saying these things when you may think another, but you are not a hypocrite. What you are doing is choosing to rise to whom you really are in Christ and to what you are really called to do. Let's ask God to help us be the best version of who we are.

Ask him for patience, to wait on his perfect plans.

Ask him for gentleness, to receive good things from his hand.

Ask him for self-control, to quit pining for someone else's life.

You and I?

We don't have to let jealousy run rampant in our lives.

We can choose to honor God.

We can choose to get glory for God.

simple steps

To close out session 3, I want to give you some simple steps you can take to begin implementing your newfound awareness of how you're spending your time and—by extension—your life.

☐ **Read 1 Chronicles 29:10–13 each day.** This is the same benediction I read to you at the close of this session's video. I'll include it word for word in the quotebox for easy access. Sit with these ideas. Think carefully on these ideas. Let this reminder of God's goodness, God's graciousness, God's incomparable power, frame how you walk through your days.

> "Praise be to you, LORD,
>   the God of our father Israel,
>   from everlasting to everlasting.
> Yours, LORD, is the greatness and the power
>   and the glory and the majesty and the
>   splendor,
>   for everything in heaven and earth is yours.
> Yours, LORD, is the kingdom;
>   you are exalted as head over all.
> Wealth and honor come from you;
>   you are the ruler of all things.
> In your hands are strength and power
>   to exalt and give strength to all.
> Now, our God, we give you thanks,
>   and praise your glorious name.

☐ **Encourage someone who is giving glory to God.** If you catch someone honoring God in her actions or words, tell her that you noticed and that you think the move was *great*. If you don't know the person directly, then you can at least repost the occurrence or tell others face to face. "I just love how (so-and-so) turned the attention from herself to God," you might say. "I want to be more like that." We need some more hyped-up people in the world! That is the kind of world I want to be a part of.

☐ **Practice giving glory to God.** Many people are naturals at giving compliments, but how many of us give them in a way that honors God? Between now and when you work through session 4, practice complimenting others in a God-glorifying manner. Practice directing the praise to him. Here are some examples of how to make the shift, in case you're ready to give it a try:

- Instead of saying, "You are so sweet!" try saying, "I praise God for your kindness."

- Instead of saying, "Thanks for helping me with that project," try saying, "I thank God for your spirit of service and helpfulness. Your friendship is a gift to me from him."

- Instead of saying, "I'm doing well! Thanks for asking," try saying, "God has been really gracious to me lately. I see his fingerprints all over my life right now . . ."

- Instead of saying, "Things have been tough . . ." try saying, "I'm trusting God on a moment-by-moment basis today! I know he will see me through."

say grace

[Based on Chapters 7 & 8]

If we can't believe that God's grace really does cover our mistakes, really does forgive our sins, really does invite us to keep going, really does empower us with strength, then how in the world are we going to help other people believe those things?

—srh

this sesh

Read this quietly to yourself before getting started.

God has good plans for your life.

I want to say that again: God has good plans for your life. If I could imprint one thing on the inside of your eyelids and mine, one thing that we would see whenever we closed our eyes in fear or in frustration or in shame, it would be that singular truth: *God has good plans for your life.*

In this session, we'll explore this reality. We'll also look at what happens when because of our selfishness or sinfulness—or both—we totally botch those plans. Do we somehow forfeit God's dreams for us? Do we lose out on all he intended for us?

If the point of session 2—"Choose Love Over Likes"—was to remind you that you are deeply loved, then the point of this session is to convince you that you'll *always* be deeply loved. Regardless of what you do. Regardless of what you don't do. Regardless of how utterly and completely you mess up God's beautiful plans.

settling in

Group leader, read this note from Sadie aloud.

How are you feeling about these three-minute experiments in pausing life and silencing yourself in the presence of God? Getting any easier to accomplish the sitting-still part? I hope so—for you and me both!

During this session we will be talking about the subject of *grace*. Just out of curiosity, how would you define grace? Culturally, if we were to describe a friend as *graceful*, we might mean that she is as coordinated as a ballet dancer or as elegant as a Golden Age movie star. To say a friend is *gracious* might mean that he is compassionate or that he has a certain generosity of spirit. But in the Christian faith, grace means something far different from all of that. Even the dictionary gets the theology of this word right. In terms of defining the noun *grace*, Merriam-Webster's very first entry says:

> *"Unmerited divine assistance given to humans for their regeneration or sanctification;*
>
> *a virtue coming from God; a state of sanctification enjoyed through divine assistance."* [3]

By the way, if you are ever having a spiritual conversation with a friend who isn't sure she believes that the Bible is the Word of God, consider using a dictionary website for your evangelistic tool! You'll find great definitions for everything from creation and Satan and sin to confession and redemption and grace, from God and Jesus and the Holy Spirit to salvation and restoration and joy. Give it a try!

---

3 Grace | Definition of Grace by Merriam-Webster

But back to our topic at hand. Grace is unmerited favor from God. Someone once said that the letters in the word "grace" could stand for "God's Riches At Christ's Expense." Because of grace, in other words, you and I can gain access to the resources of our heavenly Father. And how is that grace made available to us? By the work of Christ on the cross.

Here's how the apostle Paul says it, in a letter he wrote to the believers at Ephesus to encourage them in their faith and to call them to unity in Christ:

> For it is by grace you have been saved, through faith—and this is not from yourselves, it is the gift of God—not by works, so that no one can boast. For we are God's handiwork, created in Christ Jesus to do good works, which God prepared in advance for us to do.
>
> — Ephesians 2:8-10).

So many important ideas packed into so few verses there, right? As always, feel free to meditate on any word or phrase that resonates with you from that passage. As I think about the concepts Paul presented, here are a few that jumped to my mind:

- ☐ Thank you, Lord, for grace!
- ☐ I have been saved by grace.
- ☐ We are saved by grace through faith.
- ☐ Grace is a gift.
- ☐ Thank you, God, for grace.
- ☐ You have good works for me to do.
- ☐ You have prepared good works for me.
- ☐ Help me boast only in your grace.
- ☐ Grace
- ☐ Faith

Timer set for three minutes?
Aaand,

Go.

Sadie

roll tape

Watch the video for Session 4: "Say Grace" (about 15 minutes). Use the space below to log your thoughts, notes, and quotes you don't want to forget.

When things don't go according to plan

God has very good plans for us

The broken, fallen scene

In a perfect world, you and I would be born into a reality that didn't include fallenness, or brokenness, or distance from God. It would be sin-free. Wouldn't that be something? Totally and utterly sin-free. Amazing. And yet: You've probably noticed by now that we didn't arrive onto that scene.

Is there any hope for us at all?

On wearing shame like a coat

Grace says, "I'll never cancel you"

Are we winning arguments or winning hearts?

whatcha think?

Work through the following questions with your group (or on your own) based on the video you just watched. If you're short on time, choose to engage only with the questions that seem most relevant to you or your group.

1 **Were you able to relate to my birth story, where it felt like absolutely nothing went according to plan? When have you had a carefully strategized set of circumstances run totally haywire for you? How did that derailing make you feel?**

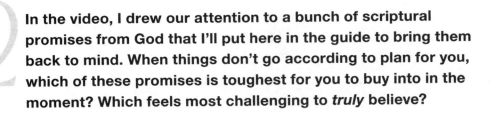

2 **In the video, I drew our attention to a bunch of scriptural promises from God that I'll put here in the guide to bring them back to mind. When things don't go according to plan for you, which of these promises is toughest for you to buy into in the moment? Which feels most challenging to *truly* believe?**

☐ **Proverbs 3:6.** "In all your ways, submit to him [God], and he will make your paths straight."

☐ **Psalm 32:8.** "I [God] will instruct you and teach you in the way you should go; I will counsel you with my loving eye on you."

☐ **Romans 8:28–30.** "And we know that in all things God works for the good of those who love him, who have been called according to his purpose. For those God foreknew he also predestined to be conformed to the image of his Son, that he might be the firstborn among many brothers and sisters. And those he predestined, he also called; those he called, he also justified; those he justified, he also glorified."

☐ **Ephesians 2:10.** "For we are God's handiwork, created in Christ Jesus to do good works, which God prepared in advance for us to do."

We have a huge problem in our world today, and it's only getting worse. We're fighting more to win arguments than to win each other's hearts. The problem with this trend? Following Jesus doesn't mean ostracizing "certain kinds" of people. Following Jesus means loving *all* people well.

3 **Sometimes we blame God for things not panning out the way they were "supposed" to, and sometimes we know it's our own fault that the threads of our world are unraveling and pooling in a giant mound at our feet.**

Can you relate? No need to share the specifics, if you're going through this study with a group. Rather, simply answer this question instead: What emotions do you suspect the apostle Paul was feeling as he penned the now-famous words of Romans 7:15–20? (See quotebox for complete text.)

> " I do not understand what I do. For what I want to do I do not do, but what I hate I do. And if I do what I do not want to do, I agree that the law is good. As it is, it is no longer I myself who do it, but it is sin living in me. For I know that good itself does not dwell in me, that is, in my sinful nature. For I have the desire to do what is good, but I cannot carry it out. For I do not do the good I want to do, but the evil I do not want to do—this I keep on doing. Now if I do what I do not want to do, it is no longer I who do it, but it is sin living in me that does it.
>
> — Romans 7:15–20 "

4 Despite what God says about us and over us and to us, why are we prone to assuming that whenever we make mistakes, God sees us in the same disparaging way that we tend to see ourselves—that he is frustrated with us, and then angry with us, and then resentful of us, and then totally ashamed to be associated with us at all?

5 As I mentioned in the video, after we spend enough time in this awful frustration-anger-resentment-shame downward spiral, this weird dynamic takes hold of us where we believe we've ventured beyond the boundaries of grace. We see how very holy God is. We see how very sinful we are. And we start wondering if the gap is just too wide to ever be bridged. We wonder if God should just cancel us and get on with his life.

Ever been true for you? If so, what assumptions were you making about God's feelings toward you that he has *never once stated* were true?

I claimed in the video that the reason we "say grace" over our missteps and mistakes is because grace is the only thing that can stop our freefall, when we're falling-down mad at life. What did you make of this section? When have you found these ideas to be true?

We're going to trip and fall.
We're going to fumble the ball.
We're going to try and fail.
We're going to botch the whole thing sometimes.

But if we can simply learn to recenter our thoughts on grace,
we'll be able to begin again.

How do the words of Romans 3:20–24 (see quotebox) bear out this idea that it is grace that helps us to begin anew, time and time again?

Therefore no one will be declared righteous in God's sight by the works of the law; rather, through the law we become conscious of our sin. But now apart from the law the righteousness of God has been made known, to which the Law and the Prophets testify. This righteousness is given through faith in Jesus Christ to all who believe. There is no difference between Jew and Gentile, for all have sinned and fall short of the glory of God, and all are justified freely by his grace through the redemption that came by Christ Jesus.

— Romans 3:20-24

Do you agree or disagree with the idea that "the reason we cancel each other so easily is because we have been practicing so long on ourselves"? Why?

What might happen to our rampant "cancel culture" if more people believed they were completely forgiven by God, and if they could completely forgive themselves?

constructive convos

Read the conversation starters below, think through how you'd finish one or two of the sentences, and then take turns completing the sentences with the whole group. See if you can make it a few rounds. Be sure to carve out time for each group member to respond to at least one prompt.

Note: If you're doing this section solo, then consider having a few of the following conversations with family members, neighbors, work associates, or friends sometime this week OR just journal your responses in some alone time.

What I'd say "grace" means to me is . . .	A time when I really experienced the power of God's grace was . . .	It's toughest for me to receive the grace of God when . . .
Sometimes I wonder if when God looks at me he sees . . .	I wish I could see in myself the (_____) that God says he sees in me.	I'd characterize my experience with shame as . . .
To me, shame feels like . . .	I wish that instead of feeling shame for the things I've done, I could feel . . .	To me, God's promise that in him I am a new creation means . . .

workin' it out on your own

Spend time on your own between videos and group meetings to work through some more personal questions.

One of the best ways to stay in touch both with our need for grace and with God's constant flow of grace toward our lives is to tell our "God story" as often as we can. If you read the book that inspired this study, *Who Are You Following?*, then you know that my husband, Christian, had a radical experience with God one night in college after shotgunning beers on a balcony at a frat party. He walked home in the rain from that night, knelt on the floor of his room, and told God that he didn't want to live that way anymore. He went from darkness to light in an instant! It was amazing, this work of the Lord.

Now, everyone doesn't have a God story as dramatic as this one. But my guess is that you do have a story to tell. If you're living for Jesus today, then odds are there was a time you can remember when you *absolutely weren't living that way*. My question for you is how *were* you living? What *was* true of your life?

If you were to craft your own before-and-after story, how would you put words to each of those things?

Maybe you were annoyingly judgmental and legalistic.
Maybe you were a partier, like Christian was.
Maybe you faked your way through every interaction.
Maybe in most of your key relationships, you were selfish and distant and cold.

Maybe you were jealous, envious, and controlling.
Maybe you were living in lust or sexual sin.

But then?

Then you met Jesus.

And things started to change from there.

Listen, you know as well as I do that just because we "surrender our lives to Jesus," we don't stop sinning once and for all. And we certainly don't stop being tempted. (Although if that program were available to us, I'd be first in line to sign up.) But equally true is that the minute we know Christ, our hearts start leaning more toward him. We start wanting what he wants. We start loving what he loves. We start aiming for his definition of excellence.

That new direction is what I'm calling the "after" state. It doesn't mean we've arrived, by any means. It just shows that we're on a new course. *We're becoming* more compassionate. *We're becoming* more self-controlled. *We're becoming* more authentic. *We're becoming* warmer with those we love.

So: Your turn. If you were to articulate your before-and-after "God story," how would you do it? Go on: Give it a try! Just complete the prompts, below.

I used to be . . .

But then I met Jesus when I . . .

And now I . . .

When you think through your God story and practice telling your God story, you remind everyone listening—including yourself!—that no matter what happened to you in your past, God has a good future in store for you. Despite the wrongs that occurred back then, God still loves you here and now.

When other people hear you talk in this way, they begin to believe these truths for themselves. You give them permission to be real about the pain they have known and about the grace they have found in God. You remind them that every one of us has fallen terribly short of the glory of God (read Romans 3:23) and that *God chooses to fight for us still.*

simple steps

To close out session 4, I want to offer up some simple steps you can take to begin watching for ways in everyday life to gather more and more glory for God.

☐ **Focus on grace this week.** Write the word on a sticky note and put it on the mirror where you get dressed every morning. Create a new screensaver with just that reminder: *grace.* Grab a Sharpie and give yourself a semi-permanent tattoo. Whatever you do, think about grace. Talk about grace. Praise God for his grace in your life. What we water grows, right? Water some grace this week.

☐ **Tell your story!** Practice with a trusted friend or family member, if that will embolden you to go tell your story out in the wild. We are actually called to confess. It is part of our walking in spiritual freedom. Go tell your testimony. Hear the words as they come out of your mouth. Watch your heart expand as you recount God's goodness to you from darkness to light. And thank him as he uses your testimony to give people comfort and confidence and hope.

> We can't give away what we don't possess. We can't help guide our friends and family to a place we've never been. We must take this first baby step: We have to let grace start marking our days.

☐ **Dare to dream.** In John Newton's beloved eighteenth-century hymn "Amazing Grace," this line appears: "'Tis grace hath brought me safe thus far, and grace will lead me home." Grace really has brought us safely to where we're sitting today. Isn't that incredible? Despite all the struggles we never thought we'd emerge from, here we are, friend. Here we are. The question now is this: Where will grace lead you next? What battle do you pray will be won? What issue do you pray will resolve? What pain do you pray will be lifted? What relationship do you pray will be healed? Go ahead and ask God now for his grace to lead you to that next steppingstone of growth. Grace has brought you safely here! May God's grace lead you home.

refuse to just "do you"

[Based on Chapter 9]

When we follow our hearts, things get risky. When we follow Jesus, we're totally safe.

—srh

this sesh

Read this quietly to yourself before getting started.

What the world says is this: "Follow your heart."

What the world says is this: "Live your best life."

What the world says is this: "You do you, boo."

What the world says is this: "Be true to yourself."

What the world says is this: "Live your truth."

What the world will say: "Follow your feelings."

What Jesus says: "Die to yourself and follow me."

Quite the opposite, as you can see.

In this session, we'll look at which path is more fulfilling—the world's way, or the way of Christ. No surprise here: It's only by going God's way that we'll find the satisfaction we seek.

settling in

Group leader, read this note from Sadie aloud.

Your fifth and final opportunity to be still and know that God is God has arrived! Well, the final one for this study, anyway. I hope you've been so awestruck over what God can do in the mind and heart of one of his daughters in a mere three minutes that you'll make this a go-forward practice in your life. But listen, whether you practice this at the same time every day, or you simply tuck it away for future use whenever the thought occurs to you, know that any time spent in the presence of God is time really, really well spent.

You know how you feel when someone you adore reaches out with a text or a call, right? Our heavenly Father feels the same way! Each time you and I stop what we're doing, put down whatever we're holding in our hands—which always includes our phones, right?—and sit quietly in his presence just pondering his goodness in our lives . . . I think he takes great delight in. I can only imagine the joy God must feel.

Now, since we're already on the subject of spending time alone with our heavenly Father, let me introduce our topic for this session: *unity with God*. Fitting, right? We will look at what it means to be women who don't just *say* we are followers of Jesus but who are *actually following him*. Women who aren't just *claiming* to spend time with our heavenly Father, but who are *actually doing just that*.

Ready for the passage I'd like to invite you to focus on during your three minutes of quiet meditation today? It is recorded in John 17:20–23 that Jesus says:

> 'My prayer is not for them alone. I pray also for those who will believe in me through their message, that all of them may be one, Father, just as you are in me and I am in you. May they also be in us so that the world may believe that you have sent me. I have given them the glory that you gave me, that they may be one as we are one—I in them and you in me—so that they may be brought to complete unity. Then the world will know that you sent me and have loved them even as you have loved me.'
>
> —John 17:20-23

A few words and phrases you might put on repeat in your mind:

- ☐ Help me be one with you, Father.
- ☐ May the world know you as God.
- ☐ Unity
- ☐ Peace
- ☐ Togetherness in the body of Christ
- ☐ You have loved us.
- ☐ Thank you for your love, God.
- ☐ May I be known as one who lives "in you."
- ☐ Help me stay in you all day.

Once you set your timer for three minutes,

feel free to
Begin.

Sadie

roll tape

Watch the video for Session 5: "Refuse to Just 'Do You'" (about 17 minutes). Use the space below to log your thoughts, notes, and quotes you don't want to forget.

Scrolling Jesus' feeds

Deny yourself to follow him

The lie of "you do you"

Unless "myself" is surrendered fully to Someone greater than me, being "true to myself" is a crazy-making experience. Why? Because "myself" can change every day. Sometimes every hour! She has ups. She has downs. She can be petty and impulsive and rude. She flits from one thing to another. She has been known to be jealous from time to time.

Notes continued ▶

Jesus, to us: "Trust me"

Losing our life to find it

"I in them and you in me"

Talking to God

Resting in God's love

whatcha think?

Work through the following questions with your group (or on your own) based on the video you just watched. If you're short on time, choose to engage only with the questions that seem most relevant to you or your group.

Out of curiosity, have you ever tried "just doing you" in a given situation? What did that look like, and how did things turn out?

As I mentioned in the video, Jesus has *expectations* about what it takes to follow him. (See quotebox for a quick refresher of what I said.) What do you make of his steep entrance fee?

> This Jesus is the same one who told his first-century followers to leave their mothers and fathers and sisters and brothers and extended families and friendship groups and hard-won businesses and hard-earned cash and come and follow him. "Die to yourself," he even said to each one. Why? Because he knew they wouldn't need it anymore.

Take another look at the words to Psalm 37, the same psalm I read onscreen. What are the actions that as believers we are to take, and what are the promised results in our lives when we take them? Complete the grid on the next page. I've provided an example to get you going.

ACTIONS WE'RE TO TAKE	PROMISED RESULTS WHEN WE DO
Ex. Trust in the Lord.	*It will all work out.*

4 **Do you agree or disagree with the statement I made that "whatever you and I are looking for as we endlessly, mindlessly, fruitlessly scroll our feeds will be found only in the person of Jesus? And as we begin to call off all those other searches, real fulfillment will begin to unfold"?**

What might this idea have to do with Jesus asking for such devotion from everyone who would follow him?

What do you learn from John 6:68 (see quotebox) about where real life is truly found?

Simon Peter answered him, 'LORD, to whom shall we go? You have the words of eternal life.'

—John 6:68

When have you experienced what we might call "spiritual fulfillment"? What were the circumstances involved, and why was the occasion so memorable for you?

constructive convos

Read the conversation starters below, think through how you'd finish one or two of the sentences, and then take turns completing the sentences with the whole group. See if you can make it a few rounds. Be sure to carve out time for each group member to respond to at least one prompt.

Note: If you're doing this section solo, then consider having a few of the following conversations with family members, neighbors, work associates, or friends sometime this week OR just journal your responses in some alone time.

I'm most fulfilled when I am . . .	Should I trust myself? I'd say . . .	To me, trusting Jesus means . . .
When I think about "losing my life," I think about . . .	I'd describe my prayer life these days as . . .	I'm especially drawn to Scripture when . . .
I'm most tempted to go my own way when . . .	The kindest person I know is . . .	The type of spiritual fruit I hope I can bear someday is . . .

workin' it out on your own

Spend time on your own between videos and group meetings to work through some more personal questions.

The focus of this entire study has been helping us become more intentional about the voices we're allowing to influence our attitudes and assumptions, our actions and reactions, our habits and hang-ups, the thoughts we think and the words we say, and our ability to love God well.

For this final Q&A segment, I'd like to invite you to carve out a few minutes, get away somewhere on your own, and ponder three questions with me. You read that right: Three little questions! How hard can that be?

I should mention that these questions are deep—*super* deep.

Yet, the benefit of you answering these questions will have a greater impact on your life than you realize. What these questions are designed to do is to align your desires with God's desires.

Ready for the three questions?

1 **Based on all that you know and all that you've learned in this study, what is most important to the heart of your heavenly Father? What's most valuable to him?**

2

Based on everything you're involved with today—online and in real life—what is most important to *your* heart? What's most valuable to you?

3

What might you lose if you adopted God's list as your own? More importantly, what might you gain?

simple steps

To close out session 5, I want to offer some simple steps you can take to begin to trust Jesus' way day by day.

Look up and meditate on the truths about Jesus. Look up each entry below in your Bible, and then jot down on the lines beneath it the truth or truths it holds.

- **Philippians 2:8** _____

    _____

    _____

- **Ephesians 4:32** _____

    _____

    _____

- **1 John 4:8** _____

    _____

    _____

What's the effect of learning about our Savior? What's the benefit of focusing your attention on him?

☐ **Revisit page 90 in this guide.** What aspect of Jesus do you most see reflected in the vision you hold for yourself? Spend a few minutes in prayer, thanking God for his perfect Son, Jesus, the one who manifests every character quality we desire.

> You can follow Jesus more closely than you follow anyone else. You can become more and more like him.

☐ **Ask God for the chance to grow.** Ask God specifically for an opportunity that will help you grow in the area you revisited in the action item above. Fair warning: God loves to answer this prayer! When we ask God to let us join him in his work, guess what he does? *He lets us join him in his work.* So, don't ask for the chance to grow with God unless you're actually prepared to grow. But if you are, then get ready! God will send you that opportunity *for sure.* You just have to be willing to step in.

tomorrow &
the day after that

As you move forward with fresh awareness of who you're following and why, I want to remind you of five considerations that will help you stay your course. What follows is an adaptation of the "Follower Reset" at the back of the book, *Who Are You Following?* Scan the categories and see how you'd answer the questions today. Then trust God to help shape the answers that best honor him on all the tomorrows after that.

consideration 1: who?

- Who do you want to influence your life?
- Who encourages and inspires you?
- Who points you toward Jesus consistently?
- Who is stopping your growth?
- Who makes you feel good about yourself?
- Who plants doubt in your heart?
- Who remains optimistic, even when things get hard?
- Who drags you down every time?

consideration 2: which?

- Which apps, platforms, podcasts, and shows are useful to your spiritual growth?
- Which apps, platforms, podcasts, and shows just aren't?

consideration 3: where?

- Where do you presently engage with online content?
- Where might you engage with online content so that you can avoid endless scrolling?

consideration 4: when?

- When do you currently engage with online content?
- When is the best time to engage with online content?
- When do you connect with real-life friends and family members? Do you protect this time consistently?
- When will you decide to make the changes you know you need to make?

consideration 5: why?

- Why are you following the people and groups you're following? What are you getting from them?
- Why are you on social media? Why do you generally post?
- Why are you postponing necessary changes to the voices influencing your life? What assumptions or fears are standing in your way, and how might your heavenly Father help counter those?

COMPANION BOOK TO ENRICH YOUR STUDY EXPERIENCE

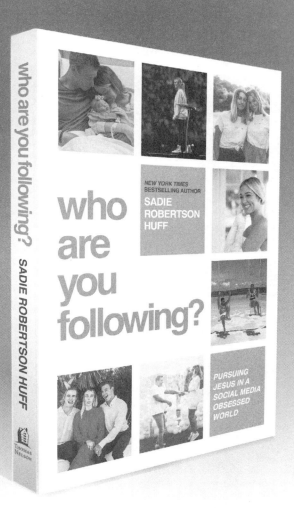

ISBN 9780785289913

Available wherever books are sold

From the Publisher

GREAT STUDIES

ARE EVEN BETTER WHEN THEY'RE SHARED!

Help others find this study:

- Post a review at your favorite online bookseller.

- Post a picture on a social media account and share why you enjoyed it.

- Send a note to a friend who would also love it—or, better yet, go through it with them.

Thanks for helping others grow their faith!